P9-ARV-059

The publishers are grateful for permission to reproduce the following material:

Poems from *Out and About* by Shirley Hughes, copyright © 1988 by Shirley Hughes. Reprinted by permission of Lothrop, Lee & Shepard Books, a division of William Morrow and Company, Inc.

Illustrations from *Michael Foreman's Mother Goose:* Copyright © 1991 by Michael Foreman, reproduced by permission of Harcourt Brace & Company.

Poems from *Clap Your Hands* edited by Sarah Hayes, illustrated by Toni Goffe. Text: Copyright © 1988 by Sarah Hayes. Illustrations: Copyright © 1988 by Toni Goffe. Reprinted by permission of Lothrop, Lee & Shepard Books, a division of William Morrow and Company, Inc.

"Clap Hands," reprinted with the permission of Little Simon, an imprint of Simon & Schuster Children's Publishing Division, from *Clap Hands* by Helen Oxenbury. Copright © 1987 by Helen Oxenbury.

"Tickle, Tickle," reprinted with the permission of Little Simon, an imprint of Simon & Schuster Children's Publishing Division, from *Tickle, Tickle* by Helen Oxenbury. Copyright © 1987 by Helen Oxenbury.

"All Fall Down," reprinted with the permission of Little Simon, an imprint of Simon & Schuster Children's Publishing Division, from *All Fall Down* by Helen Oxenbury. Copyright © 1987 by Helen Oxenbury.

"Say Goodnight," reprinted with the permission of Little Simon, an imprint of Simon & Schuster Children's Publishing Division, from *Say Goodnight* by Helen Oxenbury. Copyright © 1987 by Helen Oxenbury.

"Remember" by Pamela Mordecai copyright © 1987 by Ginn & Company Ltd. from *Storypoems – A First Collection* reproduced with the permission of Ginn & Company Ltd.

Rhymes from *Arnold Lobel's Mother Goose:* Copyright © 1986 by Arnold Lobel. Reprinted by arrangement with Random House, Inc.

Poems from *A Cup of Starshine: Poems and Pictures for Young Children:* "Naughty Soap Song" by Dorothy Aldis reprinted by permission of G. P. Putnam's Sons from *All Together* copyright 1925–1928, 1934, 1939, 1952, © renewed 1953–1956, 1962, 1967 by Dorothy Aldis.

Illustrations from *A Cup of Starshine: Poems and Pictures for Young Children:* Copyright © 1991 by Graham Percy, reproduced by permission of Harcourt Brace & Company.

Poems from *Stamp Your Feet* edited by Sarah Hayes, illustrated by Toni Goffe. Text: Copyright © 1988 by Sarah Hayes. Illustrations copyright © 1988 by Toni Goffe. Reprinted by permission of Lothrop, Lee & Shepard Books, a division of William Morrow and Company, Inc.

"The Monster Stomp" from *Stamp Your Feet,* A & C Black (Publishers) Ltd. in association with Inter-Action Imprint for the first verse of "The Monster Stomp" by John Perry from *Game-Songs with Prof Dogg's Troupe.*

First U.S. edition 1996

Library of Congress Cataloging-in-Publication Data
The Candlewick book of first rhymes.
Summary: An anthology of poetry featuring works from classic Mother Goose
to original poems and illustrations by artists such as Maurice Sendak,
Helen Oxenbury, and Shirley Hughes.
ISBN 0-7636-0015-6
1. Children's poetry, American. [1. American poetry—Collections.]
PS586.3.C36   1996
811.008'09282—dc20   95-49928

2 4 6 8 10 9 7 5 3 1

Printed in Italy

Candlewick Press
2067 Massachusetts Avenue
Cambridge, Massachusetts 02140

THE
CANDLEWICK
BOOK OF
FIRST
RHYMES

DISCARD

CANDLEWICK PRESS
CAMBRIDGE, MASSACHUSETTS

CONTENTS

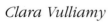
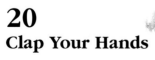

Out and About

Shirley Hughes

Sand

I like sand.
The run-between-your-fingers kind,
The build-it-into-castles kind.
Mountains of sand meeting the sky,
Flat sand, going on for ever.
I *do* like sand.

Water

I like water.

The shallow,
  splashy,
    paddly kind,

The hold-on-tight-it's-deep kind.

Slosh it out of buckets,
Spray it all around.

I *do* like water.

Wind

I like the wind.
The soft, summery, gentle kind,
The gusty, blustery, fierce kind.
Ballooning out the curtains,
Blowing things about,
Wild and wilful everywhere.
I *do* like the wind.

Mud

I like mud.

The slippy, sloppy, squelchy kind,
 The slap-it-into-pies kind.

Stir it up in puddles,
 Slither and slide.

I *do* like mud.

Monkeys on the Bed

illustrated by Chris Riddell

Three little monkeys
Jumping on the bed;
One fell off
And bumped his head.

Momma called the doctor,
The doctor said:
"No more monkeys
Jumping on the bed."

Michael Foreman's

RING-A-RING O' ROSES

Ring-a-ring o' roses,
A pocket full of posies,
  A-tishoo! A-tishoo!
We all fall down.

The cows are in the meadow,
Lying fast asleep,
  A-tishoo! A-tishoo!
We all get up again.

Mother Goose

GOOSE FEATHERS

Cackle, cackle, Mother Goose,
Have you any feathers loose?
Truly have I, pretty fellow,
Half enough to fill a pillow.
Here are quills, take one or two,
And down to make a bed for you.

LITTLE BIRD

Once I saw a little bird
  Come hop, hop, hop;
So I cried, Little bird,
  Will you stop, stop, stop?

I was going to the window
  To say, How do you do?
But he shook his little tail,
  And far away he flew.

JERRY HALL

Jerry Hall
He is so small,
A rat could eat him,
Hat and all.

15

HERE COME THE
BABIES

Catherine *and* **Laurence Anholt**

What do babies look like?

Wriggles and dribbles and sticking-out ears,
Little round faces with rivers of tears.
Babies wear suits which are long at the toes,
They stick out in the middle and up at the nose.

What do babies play with?

Pom-poms and bows, fingers and toes,
Shoes and hats, sleeping cats,
Frizzy hair, saggy bear,
Empty box, Daddy's socks.

What do lots of babies do?

One baby bouncing on her brother's knee,
Two in a playpen, three by the sea,
Four babies yelling while their mommies try to talk,
Five babies holding hands, learning how to walk.

Yum Yum!

Bread for the ducks—
quack quack quack.

Bread for the goose—
better stand back.

Milk for the cat—
lap lap lap.

A worm for the bird—
see him flap.

Clara Vulliamy

A picnic for toys under a tree.
A drink for teddy on my knee.

Lunch is ready! Yum, yes please—
sandwich, banana, yogurt, and cheese!

Let's have a party just us two—
a bite for me, a bite for you.

In my hair,
on my nose,

load up a spoonful—
in it goes!

CLAP YOUR HANDS

Good Things to Eat

Will you have
a cookie,

Or a piece
of pie,

Or a striped
candy stick?

Well, so
will I.

Knock at the Door

Knock at the door.   Peep in.   Lift the latch.   And walk in.

Chin chopper, chin chopper, chin chopper, chin.

20

Action Rhymes *illustrated by* Toni Goffe

In a Cottage

In a cottage
in a wood

A little old man
at the window stood.

Saw a rabbit
running by

Knocking
at the
window.

"Help me!
Help me! Help!"
he said,

"Lest the
huntsman shoot
me dead."

"Come little rabbit,
Come to me,
Happy you shall be."

21

Sugarcake Bubble
and other rhymes
by Grace Nichols
illustrated by Cynthia Jabar

SUGARCAKE BUBBLE

Sugarcake, sugarcake
Bubbling in a pot,
Bubble, bubble sugarcake
Bubble thick and hot.

Sugarcake, sugarcake
Spice and coconut,
Sweet and sticky
Brown and gooey,

I could eat the lot.

HIPPITY-HIPPITY-HATCH

Hippity-Hippity-Hatch
My black fowl's on her patch
Keeping her eggs
All cozy and warm
Hippity-Hippity-Hatch.

Hippity-Hippity-Hatch
My black fowl's left her patch
Her chicks have all cracked
Into the world
Hippity-Hippity-Hatch.

TUMBLE DRYING

Spin Spin Spin
Tumble tumble tumble
Short and tall
Big and small
All go round and round.

Spin Spin Spin
Tumble tumble tumble
Nylon and cotton
Zip-up and button
All go round and round.

BABY RHYMES

Clap Hands

Clap hands, dance and spin,

Open wide and pop it in,

Blow a trumpet, bang a drum,

Wave to Daddy, wave to Mom.

Tickle, Tickle

Squelch, squelch, in the mud,

Splish, splash, scrub-a-dub,

Gently, gently, brush your hair,

Tickle, tickle, under there.

Helen Oxenbury

All Fall Down

Singing all together,

Running round and round,

Bouncy, bouncy, on the bed,

All fall down.

Say Goodnight

Up, down, up in the sky,

Swing low, swing high,

Bumpity, bumpity, hold on tight,

Hush, little babies, say goodnight.

Rhymes from OVER THE MOON

illustrated by

Charlotte Voake

Humpty Dumpty
Sat on a wall,
Humpty Dumpty
Had a great fall.

All the king's horses
And all the king's men
Couldn't put Humpty
     together again.

The man in the wilderness asked me,
How many strawberries grow in the sea?
I answered him, as I thought good,
As many as red herrings
grow in the wood.

27

I had a little nut tree,
  Nothing would it bear
But a silver nutmeg
  And a golden pear.
The king of Spain's daughter
  Came to visit me,
And all for the sake
  Of my little nut tree.
I skipped over water,
  I danced over sea,
And all the birds in the air
  Couldn't catch me.

Goosy, goosy gander,
Who stands yonder?
Little Betty Baker.
Take her up and shake her.

Pat-a-cake, pat-a-cake, baker's man,
Bake me a cake as fast as you can.
Pat it and prick it, and mark it with T,
Put it in the oven for Tommy and me.

THIS IS THE
BEAR

Sarah Hayes   *illustrated by* **Helen Craig**

This is the bear who fell in the bin.
This is the dog who pushed him in.

This is the man who picked up the sack.
This is the driver who would not come back.

This is the bear who went to the dump
and fell on the pile with a bit of a bump.

This is the boy who took the bus
and went to the dump to make a fuss.

This is the man in an awful grump
who searched and searched and searched the dump.

This is the bear all cold and cross
who never thought he was really lost.

30

This is the dog who smelled the smell
of a bone and a can and a bear as well.

This is the man who drove them home—
the boy, the bear, and the dog with a bone.

This is the bear neat as a pin
who would not say just where he had been.

This is the boy who knew quite well,
but promised his friend he would not tell.

And this is the boy
who woke up in the night

and asked the bear
if he felt all right—

and was very surprised
when the bear gave a shout,

"How soon can we have
another day out?"

31

TWO CARIBBEAN POEMS

REMEMBER

Remember when
the world was tall
and you were small
and legs were all
you saw?

Jumping legs
prancing legs
skipping legs
dancing legs.

Thin legs
fat legs
dog legs
cat legs.

Shoes-and-sock legs
on the rocks legs.

Standing-very-tall legs
running-all-around legs.

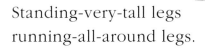

Table legs
chair legs
dark legs
fair legs.

Stooping-very-small legs
lying-on-the-ground legs.

Quick legs
slow legs
nowhere-
to-go legs.

Remember when
the world was tall
and you were small
and legs were all
you saw?

Pamela Mordecai

32

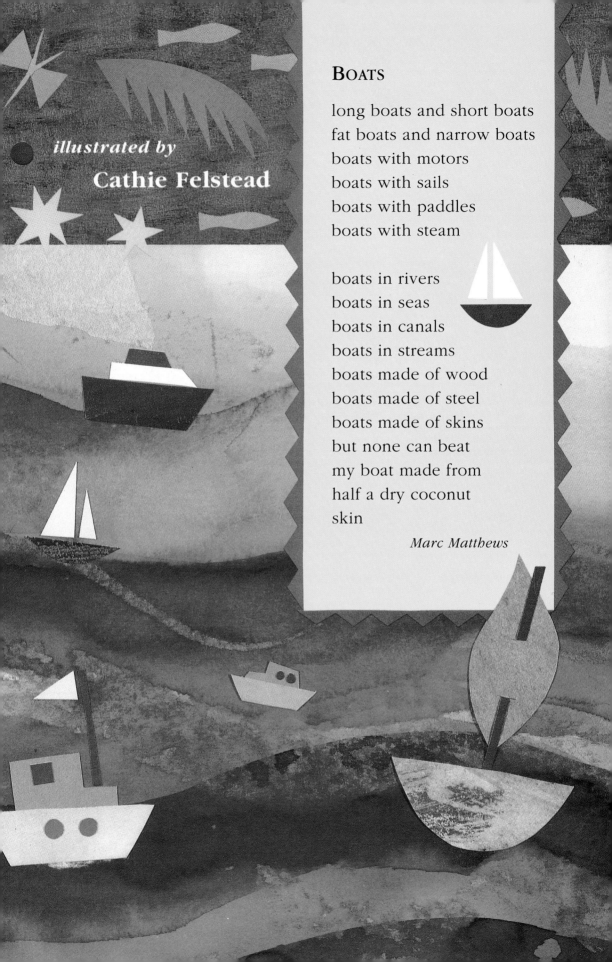

illustrated by
Cathie Felstead

BOATS

long boats and short boats
fat boats and narrow boats
boats with motors
boats with sails
boats with paddles
boats with steam

boats in rivers
boats in seas
boats in canals
boats in streams
boats made of wood
boats made of steel
boats made of skins
but none can beat
my boat made from
half a dry coconut
skin

Marc Matthews

The Train Ride

June Crebbin

illustrated by
Stephen Lambert

We're off on a journey
Out of the town—
What shall I see?
What shall I see?

Sheep running off
And cows lying down,
That's what I see,
That's what I see.

Over the meadow,
Up on the hill,
What shall I see?
What shall I see?

A mare and her foal
Standing perfectly still,
That's what I see,
That's what I see.

There is a farm
Down a bumpety road—
What shall I see?
What shall I see?

A shiny red tractor
Pulling its load,
That's what I see,
That's what I see.

Here in my seat,
My lunch on my knee,
What shall I see?
What shall I see?

    A ticket collector
    Smiling at me,
    That's what I see,
    That's what I see.

Over the treetops,
High in the sky,
What shall I see?
What shall I see?

    A giant balloon
    Sailing by,
    That's what I see,
    That's what I see.

Listen! The engine
Is slowing down—
What shall I see?
What shall I see?

    A market square,
    A seaside town,
    That's what I see,
    That's what I see.

There is the lighthouse,
The sand, and the sea . . .
Here is the station—
Whom shall I see?

    There is my grandma
    Welcoming me . . .
    Welcoming
    Me.

ARNOLD LOBEL'S
MOTHER

Rub-a-dub-dub,
Three men in a tub,
And how do you think they got there?
The butcher, the baker,
The candlestick-maker,
They all jumped out of a rotten potato,
'Twas enough to make a man stare.

Incey wincey spider
Climbed the water spout,
Down came the rain
And washed poor spider out.
Out came the sun
And dried up all the rain;
Incey wincey spider
Climbed the spout again.

Hector Protector was dressed all in green;
Hector Protector was sent to the queen.
The queen did not like him,
No more did the king;
So Hector Protector was sent back again.

36

GOOSE

Georgie Porgie, pudding and pie,
Kissed the girls and made them cry;
When the boys came out to play,
Georgie Porgie ran away.

Three blind mice, see how they run!
They all ran after the farmer's wife,
Who cut off their tails with a carving knife;
Did you ever see such a sight in your life
As three blind mice?

GOOD ZAP, LITTLE GROG

by Sarah Wilson

ZOODLE OOP

Zoodle oop, little Grog,
give a hug; stretch and yawn.
The night moons are fading.
There's shine on the lawn.

Uncurl from your covers,
you sleepy gurraff.
The ooglets are tuzzling.
(Try hard not to laugh!)

The flooms in the garden
have started to wink.
A tiny paroobie
is churling,
"Zlink-zlink!"

So hop to your glockers
and socks right away.
Zoodle oop, little Grog.
Run and play!
Run and play!

YOOP DOOZ

Yoop dooz, little Grog,
there are zoofs in the sky.
The glipneeps are jumping
and ready to fly.

The day-stars are fizzing
in polka-dot trails.
Your smibblets are giggling
and chasing their tails.

Nearby in the garden,
who's frilling for you?
A little green zibblet
in spangles—that's who!

Zoof

Frullop

ZLINK! ←Paroobie

Grib

Ooglet

Smibblet

So trok with the frullops
and chase every sun.
Yoop dooz, little Grog.
Come have fun!
Come have fun!

GOOD ZAP
Good zap, little Grog,
the moons have turned pink.
The giant chiwangas
are starting to sink.

In the dusk of the garden
a wild fribbet humms,
and all the blue zamblots
are covered in flumms.

So wave to the smuffits
and bring in your grib.
In your soft, furry nightclothes,
bounce into your crib.

Now dream with the froozels
and snuggle your feet.
Good zap, little Grog.
Go to sleep.
Go to sleep.

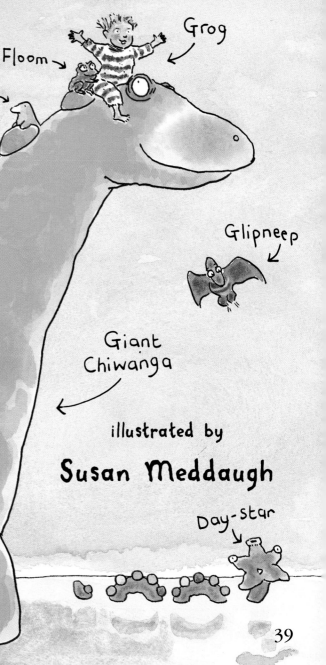

Zibblet

Floom →

Grog

Smuffit →

Zamblot

Wild fribbet

Glipneep

Froozel

Giant
Chiwanga

illustrated by
Susan Meddaugh

Day-star

39

Down at the Doctor's

Down at the doctor's,
where everybody goes,
there's a fat white cat
with a dribbly bibbly nose,
with a dribble dribble here
and a bibble bibble there,
that's the way
she dribbles her nose.

Down at the doctor's,
where everybody goes,
there's a fat black dog
with messy missy toes,
with a mess mess here
and a miss miss there,
that's the way
she messes her toes.

Down at the doctor's,
where everybody goes,
there's a fat red parrot
that everybody knows,
with a hi-de-hi here
and a how-de-how there,
that's the parrot
that everybody knows.

Messing Around

"Do you know what?"
said Jumping John.
"I had a tummyache
and now it's gone."

"Do you know what?"
said Kicking Kirsty.
"All this jumping
has made me thirsty."

"Do you know what?"
said Mad Mickey.
"I sat in some glue
and I feel all sticky."

"Do you know what?"
said Fat Fred.
"You can't see me,
I'm under the bed."

Michael Rosen   *illustrated by* **Quentin Blake**

A
CUP OF
STARSHINE

illustrated by
Graham Percy

OH, JEMIMA

Oh, Jemima,
Look at your Uncle Jim!
He's down in the duckpond
Learning how to swim.
First he's on his
Left leg,
Then he's on his
Right—

Now he's on a bar of soap,
Skidding out of
Sight!

NO HARM DONE

As I went out
The other day,
My head fell off
And rolled away.

But when I noticed
It was gone,
I picked it up
And put it on.

NAUGHTY SOAP SONG

Just when I'm ready to
Start on my ears,
That is the time that my
Soap disappears.

It jumps from my fingers and
Slithers and slides
Down to the end of the
Tub, where it hides.

And acts in a most diso-
Bedient way
AND THAT'S WHY MY SOAP'S
GROWING THINNER EACH DAY.

Dorothy Aldis

STAMP YOUR FEET

The Monster Stomp

If you want to be a monster, now's your chance
'Cause everybody's doing the monster dance.

You just stamp your feet,   Wave your arms around,

Stretch 'em up, stretch 'em up,   Then put them on the ground,

'Cause you're doing the monster stomp,
That's right, you're doing the monster stomp.
Ooh-Ah-Ooh-Ah-Ooh-Ah-Ooh-Ah!
Ooh-Ah-Ooh-Ah-Ooh-Ah-Ooh-Ah!

John Perry

Action Rhymes *illustrated by* Toni Goffe

I'm a Little Teapot

I'm a little teapot,
short and stout;
Here's my handle,
here's my spout.

When the water's boiling,
hear me shout:
"Just tip me over and
pour me out."

Hippety-hop

Hippety-hop to the baker's shop, to buy three sticks of candy.

One for you,   and one for me,   and one for sister Sandy.

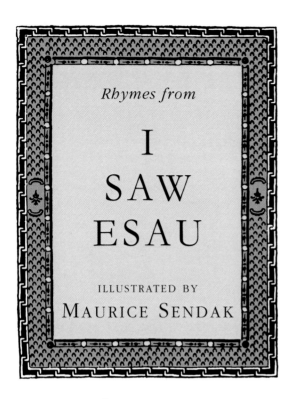

Rhymes from

I
SAW
ESAU

ILLUSTRATED BY
MAURICE SENDAK

It rains, it pains,
It patters, it docks,
It makes little ladies
Take up their white frocks.
The rain is done,
The wind is down;
Put on your best,
And go to town.

Lay the cloth, knife and fork,
Bring me up a leg of pork.
 If it's lean, bring it in,
If it's fat, take it back,
Tell the old woman I don't want that.

Nobody
loves me,

Everybody
hates me,

Going in
the garden

To-eat-
worms.

I scream,
  You scream,
  We all scream
  For ice-cream.

Mother
  made a
    seedy
      cake –

      Gave us
    all the
  belly-
  ache.

Big fat
juicy ones,

Little squiggly
niggly ones.

Going in
the garden

To-eat-
worms.

Caveman Dave and

Caveman Dave
lives in a cave—
he doesn't wash
and he doesn't shave.
He's smelly
but he's very brave.

Wild animals
don't frighten Dave—
at bears and tigers
he will wave.
Dave really is
extremely brave—

Friends!

but Dave's sister Ava
is braver!

Mrs. Pirate

Nick Sharratt

When Mrs. Pirate went shopping
she bought an apple pie
and a patch for her eye,
a bar of soap
and a telescope,
an onion and a carrot
and a red and green parrot,
underwear made to measure,
and a chest full of treasure,
buttons for her coat
and a big sailing boat,
a box full of tea,
and some sea.

MOON FROG

Richard Edwards

illustrated by **Sarah Fox-Davies**

The moon slid down the sky,
The froggy whispered, "Soon,
If only it comes close enough,
I'll leap onto the moon."

The moon slid lower still,
The froggy paused, then—hop!
His long legs launched him at the moon
And landed him on top.

The moon sailed smoothly on
Along its starry course,
With froggy proudly riding
Like a jockey on a horse.

IF I HAD A
MONSTER

Colin McNaughton

If I had a monster,
I'll tell you what I'd do.
I'd starve it for a week
And then set it on you!

53

I never saw a purple cow

and other nonsense rhymes

THE PURPLE COW

I never saw a purple cow,
I never hope to see one;
But I can tell you, anyhow,
I'd rather see than be one.

illustrated by EMMA Chichester Clark

There Was a Pig

There was a Pig, that sat alone,
   Beside a ruined pump.
By day and night he made his moan:
It would have stirred a heart of stone
   To see him wring his hoofs and groan,
Because he could not jump.

Lewis Carroll

I've Got a Dog

I've got a dog as thin as a rail,

He's got fleas all over his tail;

Every time his tail goes flop,

The fleas on the bottom all hop to the top.

Let Us Go to the Woods

Let us go to the woods, says this pig.

What to do there? says this pig.

To seek mamma, says this pig.

What to do with her? says this pig.

To kiss her, to kiss her, says this pig.

THERE WAS A RAT

There was a rat, for want of stairs,
Went down a rope
to say his prayers.

THIS PIG GOT IN THE BARN

This pig got in the barn,

This ate all the corn,

This said he wasn't well,

This said he'd go and tell,

And this said—weke, weke, weke,
I can't get over the barn door sill.

Rock-a-bye, baby,
On the treetop,
When the wind blows
The cradle will rock;
When the bough breaks
The cradle will fall,
Down will come baby,
Cradle, and all.

Diddle, diddle, dumpling,
My son John,
Went to bed
With his trousers on;
One shoe off,
And one shoe on,
Diddle, diddle, dumpling,
My son John.

MOONSHINE

illustrated by
Nicola Bayley

Come, let's to bed,
Says Sleepyhead;
Tarry awhile, says Slow.
Put on the pan,
Says Greedy Nan,
Let's sup before we go.

Rock-a-bye, baby,
Thy cradle is green;
Father's a nobleman,
Mother's a queen;
And Betty's a lady,
And wears a gold ring;
And Johnny's a drummer,
And drums for the king.

59

INDEX OF FIRST LINES

ACKNOWLEDGMENTS

page 8	"Out and About" is a selection of rhymes from the book of the same title, published by Morrow.
page 12	"Monkeys on the Bed" is taken from *Tail Feathers from Mother Goose*, edited by Iona and Peter Opie.
page 14	"Michael Foreman's Mother Goose" is a selection from the book of the same title, published by Harcourt Brace Jovanovich.
page 16	"Here Come the Babies" is a selection from the book of the same title.*
page 20	"Clap Your Hands" is a selection from the book of the same title, edited by Sarah Hayes, published by Morrow.
page 22	"Sugarcake Bubble" is a selection from *No Hickory No Dickory No Dock*, edited by John Agard and Grace Nichols.*
page 24	"Baby Rhymes" was originally published by by Macmillan as four books: *All Fall Down; Clap Hands; Say Goodnight; Tickle, Tickle*.
page 26	"Over the Moon" is a selection from the book of the same title.*
page 32	"Two Caribbean Poems" is a selection from *A Caribbean Dozen*, edited by John Agard and Grace Nichols.*
page 36	"Arnold Lobel's Mother Goose" is a selection from the book of the same title, published by Harcourt Brace Jovanovich.
page 40	"Down at the Doctor's" is taken from *Spollyollydiddlytiddlyitis – The Doctor Book*.
page 41	"Messing Around" is taken from *Under the Bed – The Bedtime Book*.
page 42	"A Cup of Starshine" is a selection from the book of the same title, edited by Jill Bennett, published by Harcourt Brace Jovanovich.
page 44	"Stamp Your Feet" is a selection from the book of the same title, edited by Sarah Hayes, published by Morrow.
page 46	"I Saw Esau" is a selection from the book of the same title, edited by Iona and Peter Opie.*
page 50	"Moon Frog" is taken from the book of the same title.*
page 52	"If I Had a Monster" is taken from *Making Friends With Frankenstein*.*
page 54	"I Never Saw a Purple Cow" is a selection from the book of the same title.
page 58	"Bedtime & Moonshine" is a selection from the book of the same title.

Throughout, where authors are not credited, they are unknown.

* Published by Candlewick Press.